RICHARD FRANKLAND is one of Australia's most experienced Indigenous singer/songwriters, authors and film makers. In 1993 Richard co-wrote and directed his first documentary with John Foss entitled *Songlines*. Since then Richard has written, directed and produced a wide range of video, documentary and film projects including the award-winning *Who Killed Malcolm Smith*, *No Way To Forget*, *After Mabo*, *Harry's War* and *Stone Bros*. Richard has also written and performed for the stage. He wrote and directed the award-winning play *Conversations with the Dead* and his stage show *An Evening with Richard Frankland* was performed at the Sydney Opera House. His latest play, *The Brady Bunch*, debuted at La Mama in 2012 and he is currently working on *Voices* for the Malthouse Theatre. *Digger*, his most recent published work, is a novel for children about the 1967 referendum and was published by Scholastic.

Photo by Caroline McCredie.

RICHARD FRANKLAND

WALKING INTO THE BIGNESS

Currency Press,
Sydney

CURRENCY PLAYS

First published in 2017
by Currency Press Pty Ltd,
PO Box 2287, Strawberry Hills, NSW, 2012, Australia
enquiries@currency.com.au
www.currency.com.au

Cataloguing-in-publication data for this title is available from the National Library of Australia website: www.nla.gov.au

Typeset by Dean Nottle for Currency Press.
Cover image by Pia Johnson. Photo shows Tammy Anderson, Paul Ashcroft, Luisa Hastings Edge, Richard Frankland, Rarriwuy Hick and Tiriki Onus. Cover design by Katy Wall for Currency Press.

Currency Press acknowledges the Traditional Owners of the Country on which we live and work. We pay our respects to all Aboriginal and Torres Strait Islander Elders, past and present.

Contents

Australian Government

Australia Council for the Arts

Publication of this title was assisted by the Commonwealth Government through the Australia Council, its arts funding and advisory body.

Richard Frankland in Malthouse Theatre's 2014 production. (Photo: Pia Johnson)

Foreword

I have known Richard for seventeen years and have known *of* him for much longer than that. He has been a mentor, a brother, and a work colleague all rolled into one.

Richard has been at the spear point of why I continue to strive to be the best artist I can. I first met Richard while performing in his play *Conversations With The Dead* in the early 2000s. My brother, Aaron Pederson, played the title role of the same play in Melbourne at the Malthouse Theatre Company and twelve months later under the direction of Wesley Enoch I was asked to be Richard in a story that encompassed an immense part of his life.

My time as an actor in this show was, in short, a life-changing experience.

The themes that Richard bled into his story were real and formidable and it had a weight to it that I had never experienced on a Western stage.

Life-changing to say the least.

I became a good friend to Richard in the years that followed and he has always been a brother that I can call upon for advice in any work or life instance and vice versa. He became family.

The next story we had to tell together was *Walking into the Bigness*. Richard and I wanted to do it again.

Malthouse Theatre Company, under the leadership of the wonderful Marion Potts, asked us if we would like to pursue the *Conversations With The Dead* story further. We said yes and were joined by another brother, Chris Mead, who came on board as co-director and all things shaping the story.

We were blessed with an extraordinary cast including Rarriwuy Hick, Paul Ashcroft, Tammy Anderson, Tiriki Onus and Luisa Hastings Edge, with the incredibly talented Monica Weightman joining Richard as our onstage musicians.

Walking into the Bigness was one of my proudest moments as a storyteller. Via the medium of Richard J. Frankland, we delivered a story that all of our audience could relate to. One did not have to be a koori living and growing up in the township of Portland, Victoria to understand the weight and substance that Richard and Chris Mead shaped. Richard gave ownership to all that came on board, and the trust we had in each other inspired all of us to engage truthfully and with an exactitude second to none.

Thank you.

Wayne Blair
May 2017

Wayne Blair is an acclaimed writer, actor, producer, and director of film, television and theatre.

Observations on Journeys, Real and Imagined

When director Wayne Blair and then-artistic director of Malthouse, Marion Potts, asked me to be a part of this work, I leapt at the chance. Having worked previously with Richard and Wayne I knew Richard's easy command of story and the generosity and inclusiveness of his vision, and Wayne's extraordinary grasp of emotional mise-en-scène and his effortlessness with actors.

It was a decade earlier, when I was Literary Manager of Sydney's Belvoir, that I had first met Wayne and Richard. Wayne was playing the central role in Richard's earlier play *Conversations with the Dead*. Under the direction of Wesley Enoch, the stellar cast included Wayne, Luke Carroll, Lillian Crombie, Elaine Crombie, Rachael Maza, Kirk Page and Vic Simms (Ralph Myers set, Mark Howett lighting, Stephanie Blake costumes and Wayne Freer music). We had the privilege of presenting the second production (after Playbox's acclaimed Melbourne presentation, led by Aaron Pederson).

We spent the first few weeks of rehearsal trimming and re-ordering the Melbourne production draft while also drawing from other texts in Richard's huge body of work – including poetry, songs and short films – all in consultation with Richard.

My involvement in this editing came under extreme scrutiny from the cast, for the good reason that I was one of the few team members who was not an Indigenous Australian. My voice was of course just one in a thoughtful, experienced and sagacious room of voices but I was representative of the coloniser, and an exponent of Western European dramaturgy. Did I have the insight or ability to help tell a story so utterly outside my learning and experience? Would I tangle and distort the narrative? Contort and mangle the storytelling? Might I be imposing a form alien to the core of this story? I might fundamentally mis-read the play then mis-diagnose possible dramaturgical solutions. Were any of my frames of reference useful or relevant? After a week or two hard at work, however, bigger questions of story and dramatic action overwhelmed us. I would come to learn and then practice the principles of Koorreen, Richard's credo: to listen, learn, and pay respect; and to act with integrity, honour, compassion and ultimately, with courage.

When we showed what we had assembled to Richard there was some trepidation from the team, because it was a significant edit. Richard, however, was undeterred. He never once put his guitar down, simply commenting: 'all change is good, all chance is proactive'. He knew that whichever way we sliced it, the play remained a detailed and authentic story about one of the most significant and shameful parts of recent Australian history, the Royal Commission into Aboriginal Deaths in Custody. Indeed it offered our audiences a brutal history of the present.

The effect of that show on audiences was palpable; and the effect on me was profound. It changed the direction of my career, brought together my rather archive-heavy degrees in Australian history with the visceral business of lived Australians and helped me see how shocking, arresting, immediate and moving theatre can be. And while I had worked with many of Australia's finest theatre practitioners before, nothing prepared me for the wisdom of Richard J. Frankland.

When starting work on the mammoth endeavour of *Walking into the Bigness*, I was handed quite a dossier. The project had begun at Belvoir and Malthouse and involved, among others, Eamon Flack as a lead researcher and interviewer. The team had already compiled interviews, scenes, ideas for scenes, poems and songs – so many songs. It was referred to as the 'Voices' Project because it was as much about Richard's travels, travails and interviews as it was about his own life – stories of oppressed, occluded, forgotten voices. Before embarking on collating or arranging any of that material however Richard invited me to his land, his house, and to meet his family.

As it turned out not only was I welcomed to Gunditjmara land, but it was a significant day – Richard's birthday. And there I was. A relative stranger. A witness again – thank you Richard – to something much bigger than I, and much more dense and complex than the thin little dramaturgy tool-book I carried with me. I was given a history lesson. A civics lesson. I met his mum. I visited sites of massacres. We stood on the shore of Portland Bay and gazed at the sea. I met his friends. I observed fierce loyalty, experienced deep listening and witnessed amazing bigheartedness. I also, later, conducted interviews of my own; receiving hours and hours of stories.

It was clear that Richard had lived at least four lives at that point. And while there was multiplicity, range and variety, there was also a clear driving force at the heart of his story. Indeed it was a field of forces that cohered his life's sprawling narrative, a field of forces that demanded a new form – a necessarily post-colonial bricolage of First Peoples' and Western modes of storytelling in writing and performance, uniting song, storytelling, dialogue, history and experience. The one sliver of his life that we could manage in one evening's performance was this: his world, worlds, of work. The work he did, the work to be done. This play would be both simple and multi-layered. We could track his life by following him from his first job in an abattoir; to his work in the army and his roving mission for the Royal Commission; his pursuit of stories of oppression and resistance in colonial war zones; and his ongoing role as mentor and guide for troubled young Indigenous men. It is a journey: chronological, aetiological and sociological.

And the two key poles in this field of forces were chaos and survival. In each moment of this play the character 'Richard' exists on the edge of chaos. We watch his body under pressure, teetering towards survival. He fights against the chaos that walks with him, chaos that he works with and through daily. Ultimately he makes himself a warrior; his war cultural, political, personal. No matter the number of times he is knocked down, Richard is guided by the necessity of work, the dignity of his mother, the grace of his father, and the certainty of his land, its rhythms and munificence. With the certainty of this spine we could get to work on the details, texture, grit and arc: 'Richard' had to work, he had to feed his family and contribute to their survival. Here, ultimately, is a strong and proud Gunditjmara man who was able to walk away from the willy-willy (or dust whilrwind) because he had to work: courageous work that would ultimately be the writing and performing itself.

This play captures the problems and possibilities of our time and does so in a formally and thematically interrogative way. Form and content are under extreme pressure but also in exquisite balance. Each scene and each moment are in balance too, harmonising dialogue, action, storytelling and song with the centripetal force of character formation and cultural purpose. Here is a journey of work, the hard work of survival, the ferocity of resistance and the beauty and joy of walking the earth, re-claimed land, home. It is a harrowing journey, a coming-of-age story. It's time for the seriousness of this hard work to be acknowledged. And told. And re-told. Shared. Discussed. And worked on. Courageously. Again. And again. That was Richard's job; now it's ours too.

Chris Mead
February 2017

Chris Mead is a director and dramaturg. He is currently the Literary Director of Melbourne Theatre Company.

Walking into the Bigness was first produced by Malthouse Theatre at the Merlyn Theatre, Melbourne, on 1 August 2014, with the following cast:

> Tammy Anderson
> Paul Ashcroft
> Luisa Hastings Edge
> Rarriwuy Hick
> Tiriki Onus

Co-directors, Wayne Blair & Chris Mead
Dramaturg, Chris Mead
Set and Costume Designers, The Sisters Hayes
Lighting Designer, Rachel Burke
Co-Musical Directors, Richard Frankland and Monica Weightman
Sound Designer, Darrin Verhagen
Choreographer, Katina Olsen
Stage Manager, Tia Clark
Assistant Stage Manager, Caitlin Byrne

CHARACTERS

RICHARD

ANNA	MAGISTRATES (3)
ARMY MATE	MEDICO
BERT	MUM
BIKIE	PASSENGER
BLINKY BILL	PUB DRUNK
BLOKES (2)	SISTERS (2)
BOYS (4)	SOLDIERS (4)
CLERK	STEEL BOSS
COLLEAGUES (2)	SURVIVOR
COPS (4)	TRUCK DRIVER
DAD	TUBBY
DANNY	UNCLE
DOCTOR	WORKMATES (4)
JUSTICE MURPHY	YOUNG RICHARD

The character of RICHARD is played by all actors. Several RICHARDS may appear onstage at the same time.

The rest of the roles are divided between the ensemble. They assume roles fluidly, with or without costume changes. A cast of five can perform this play.

/ indicates overlapping dialogue.

ACT ONE

MY LITTLE FOURTEEN-YEAR-OLD HEART

RICHARD 1: Early, early, early morning, that early that the sun is only peeping at the world, a car goes past me and the fog out of my mouth tells me it's cold; but I'm lucky it ain't raining, yet.

My little fourteen-year-old heart stops beating as a car pulls up beside me.

PASSENGER: Bothy's?

YOUNG RICHARD: Yeah.

PASSENGER: Get in, mate.

RICHARD 1: I get in and it's 1977 and we're headed to the casual shed at Borthwick's Abattoirs where every Portlander worth his salt has done his apprenticeship into the workforce of men.

The shed is packed with men, smoking, talking low, all hopeful of a job.

I light up a cigarette, immediately cough, recover, and try to look like one of the grown-ups.

BLOKE 1: That'll kill ya, mate.

BLOKE 2: Leave the kid alone, ya dickhead.

BLOKE 1: Up ya frig.

BLOKE 2: Calm down, ya crank.

RICHARD 1: Names keep getting called out; more blokes disappear, until there's only two of us left. A real skinny old bloke—so old I reckon that he was around when Jesus played halfback for Jerusalem—and me, a skinny-ankled Koori kid.

CLERK: Saunders.

RICHARD 1: I look around for a Saunders, thinking one of me cousins is here—

BERT: [*gently*] Go on, mate, it's you.

YOUNG RICHARD: [*to* BERT] I forgot.

My name's not Richard Frankland today, it's Richard Saunders, and I'm pretending I'm sixteen, not fourteen. The bloke behind the jump [*desk*] knows I'm not sixteen, he knows I've put me age up, but he knows I need the work. My dad's passed, lost my oldest brother on Good Friday, and I gotta help me mum.

CLERK: [*handing* YOUNG RICHARD *some paperwork*] The chain. [*Sighing, exasperated and gesticulating*] Outside, across to the big building, up the stairs to the kill floor, and someone will help you get in your gear.

RICHARD 1: Bothy's stinks. It smells worse than anything I have ever smelt. But it's work ... and money.

WORKMATE 1: Kid, you on the chain, are ya? Get yourself a milk crate otherwise you'll be too short to reach. I reckon they'll start you trimming—cutting off lambs' cocks.

RICHARD 1: Bloody hell, cutting off lambs' pippies—hope the sheep don't bite.

So I'm standing there, with gumboots so big the tops touch the back of my thigh.

RICHARD 2: The t-shirt sleeves touch my wrist, the pants come up to my upper chest, and the hair-holding hat is down well over my ears.

RICHARD 1: In my right hand I have a knife, a knife sharpener and scabbard that makes me look like a hobbit in a giant insane pirate's suit. In my other hand I have a milk crate and I am looking at a work floor where I can see hundreds of men, working to a chain of carcasses swinging back and forth getting skun,

RICHARD 2: chain-sawed,

RICHARD 3: sliced,

RICHARD 2: diced,

RICHARD 1: and bits and pieces being thrown into chutes to disappear into the bowels of Bothy's. And carcasses swing past fast—

RICHARD 1: I am cutting off lambs' pippies, trimming off bits of fat,

RICHARD 4: and the chain seems to go forever,

RICHARD 3: carcasses swinging in a strange dance of death.

RICHARD 1: There's a beef chain and a sheep one. Occasionally a bloke gets his metal glove caught on it, and if he's near the cog, he gets his hand mangled.

BERT: Ahhhh. Just kidding!

WORKMATE 1: You're a friggin' idiot, Bert.

RICHARD 4: Sometimes, some bloke gets bored and piffs a kidney at the back of someone's head.

RICHARD 5: It stings a bit and makes a squelchy sound.

RICHARD 2: I been hit with fish, tennis balls, rocks, but nothing quite so interesting as getting hit in the middle of the back with a kidney.

WORKMATE 2: You right, kid?

YOUNG RICHARD: Yeah …

BLINKY BILL: You're Old Chris Saunders' grandkid, hey?

YOUNG RICHARD: Yeah …

WORKMATE 3: How is the old bugger? I worked with him out here, you know.

BLINKY BILL: I picked potatoes with him.

WORKMATE 4: He was in the war with me granddad.

WORKMATE 2: Mine too, so was his cousin's brother, the one that got killed getting the medal—

WORKMATE 3: His boy, the old black captain—Old Reg Saunders—did well, hey … bloody good man.

RICHARD 1: And that bloke who was real old, the halfback for Jerusalem, Bert, says:

BERT: Your granddad worked here, right here where you're working now.

WORKMATE 3: Your pop was a dignified wag.

RICHARD 1: I'm not real sure what that is, but I remember my pop as a man with a glint in his eye and a joke on his lips.

TOUCH THE STARS

RICHARD 1: I used to sit with Granddad—Old Chris Saunders—cooking eels that we'd caught. His hands were huge. His back was straight and I thought that Pop Saunders was so tall he could touch the very stars themselves.

We caught those eels with his old mate Ray. Ray drives us out in his car to Darlots Creek. Pop wades into the water and, using a bobbin—a bobbin is worms threaded onto a line—and then when you got a mob of worms, you put a couple of snails in the middle and wrap all those worms around it, then, you tease the eel with it. The eel is a greedy fella, he takes a good gulp of that bobbin, and then once he takes hold, you flip him up onto the creek bank.

When they hit the creek bank Old Ray whacks 'em with a stick and puts 'em in the hessian bag. I fall asleep watching those two: splash, whack, splash, whack. I wake up and the car's rocking and we're chugging along a track heading back into town. I was only little then. My dad had died and Pop filled the gap for a bit.

I remember walking down the street with Pop; whitefellas would call him Mr Saunders. He would wave at them as they drove past in their cars, he would doff his hat to the ladies. He had a straight back, and to me he was so tall and strong I used to think he could shape clouds or pluck an eagle from the sky.

RICHARD 3: Seemed like everyone knew him, everyone liked him, whitefellas calling my granddad 'Mr Saunders'.

ALL: G'day, Mr Saunders.

WE TRAVEL A LOT

RICHARD 5: And I'm a Frankland too. My name's Richard Frankland

RICHARD 4: and I'm a Greek-looking Aboriginal

RICHARD 3: who's worked as a waiter in a Chinese restaurant that was owned by a white bloke who happened to be gay.

RICHARD 2: Not that there's anything wrong with being white.

RICHARD 5: The sixth Richard Frankland in a row. My dad was the fifth.

RICHARD 1: There's never much money in our house. And Mum, and my older siblings, had been incredibly poor—you know, newspapers on the walls for warmth and all that.

RICHARD 4: But with my dad we live in South Yarra and I go to Hawksburn State Primary School.

And the family we, well, then we travel a lot,

RICHARD 1: had a mob of different jobs—

RICHARD 2: Hay baling at eight. Got ripped off.

RICHARD 1: Bothy's at fourteen.

RICHARD 3: Wool baling at fifteen. Old bald Ted gets that hook in his head—

RICHARD 2: and I go to Portland South Primary for a while;

RICHARD 5: Palmer Street Primary for a little bit;

RICHARD 4: Heywood Primary for a little bit;

RICHARD 2: then sometime I went to Colac Primary, but only for a real little bit;

RICHARD 5: go to a primary school in Alice Springs—there's a couple of real bastards up there;

RICHARD 2: then Moe Primary School for a fair bit;

RICHARD 4: and then there's others, I can't remember them all.

RICHARD 2: I went to a lot of primary schools.

RICHARD 1: He was a good man, my dad. He used to teach boxing, clerk of courts. He was a non-Aboriginal man. We live in South Yarra. He says swearing is a lazy man's way of expressing himself. He says:

DAD: Have a good sense of right and wrong.

RICHARD: I love the smell of him. He's singing:

> DAD *sings a few lines of 'Zip-a-dee-doo-dah'.*

The sun's golden, the house is warm, and there's laughter everywhere, hanging in the air, everything secure and happy, strong. We are strong.

When he died, everything spun out of control.

RICHARD 3: No more songs, no more easy Dad laughter. When he went, we were easy targets for the welfare.

SIX CHILDREN

MUM: [*loud*] Come on, get your *mooms* in gear. Make your beds. Clean your beautiful teeth. Brush your hair and make sure you have shoes and socks on.

SONG: 'Cry Freedom' (instrumental underscore)

RICHARD 5: All up, my mother, Christina Saunders, had six children—a single mother of six, dealing with the non-indigenous indigenous authorities as they came into our home and judged how we lived, judging whether they would remove *her* children as they did remove some of her sister's.

MUM: Later. They did. My youngest.

RICHARD 1: Mum's dignity, the way she held herself when they looked at us like we were below them, everything about her said we were equal to the whitefellas, that we were human.

RICHARD 4: In our house, country music is king, cos it's Mum's favourite. There are no Indigenous artists on the television or on the commercial radio stations, but Lionel Rose, the world champion boxer, had released a couple of songs. Those forty-five vinyl recordings are played until almost worn out.

RICHARD 3: On Sunday mornings I see Mum singing in the kitchen, the sunlight streaming through. It's golden.

RICHARD 5: Sometimes our extended family uncles would visit and bring their guitars and the songs go on through the night.

RICHARD 1: If we're real lucky Uncle Harry Williams and the Country Outcasts drift through town and do a show—wow, what a show. One day my sister sings with The Black Opals. Uncle Johnny. Uncle Claudey Lovett. Don't ya love it?

All applaud and cheer SISTER 1 *as she goes up to the mic to sing.*

RICHARD 4: This is my big sister. She's gonna sing 'Night Moves' by Bob Seger. Listen up, you mob.

More applause and cheers. SISTER 1 *stands nervously at the mic. She turns her back to the crowd, to more cheering and laughter.*

SISTER 1 *sings some of 'Night Moves'.*

More applause and cheers.

RICHARD 5: For the whole song she didn't even turn around once. We called her The Faceless One after that.

OLD NYLON STRING GUITAR

RICHARD 4: Couple of months later, I start horsing around on an old guitar. We're a musical mob, our family.

RICHARD 1: True, aye.

RICHARD 4: We'd shifted homes. Colac.

RICHARD 1: Moe?

RICHARD 3: Heywood. Portland?

RICHARD 4: Drumborg. We're living, maybe a week, with this non-Aboriginal family. I am about eleven, twelve. And this friend of Mum's gives me this old guitar; and I use it to write my first song.

SONG: 'Gypsy Jane'

RICHARD 1: *Running through the darkness*
Searching for your lost Gypsy Jane

Played that song for hours, until my little fingers started hurting. But I kept playing though.

> *Peering into shadows*
> *Searching for your lost Gypsy Jane*

Even played it for an ethnomusicologist from Canberra who recorded it. True.

> *Where you gonna hide?*
> *Oh, when the fires burn so brightly, Gypsy Jane*
> *Oh, when the rain starts to fall, Gypsy Jane.*

Not bad for a first song, aye.

RIDING OUT OF PORTLAND

RICHARD 3: First time I try and leave Portland, Lefty Wright and my dog Keewa are running. Well, Keewa is running and me and Lefty are riding bikes, riding out of Portland; and we're loaded down with slug guns, camping gear and other provisions. Keewa's one of them dogs who does their own thing. Used to climb trees. True.

Lefty—we called him that cos his last name's Wright—he's a white kid who was adopted and lives across the road. He's a good fella, sort of angry at the world without knowing why. I was too.

We'd knocked off the town sporting goods store, we took pushbikes—neither of us had one—we took slug guns too—well, everyone wants one of them, aye? And when you're gunna hit the road that's what you need. We got other stuff as well—all of it's to take us down the highway, to escape from Portland. Got no idea what we're escaping from or where we're escaping to, but we're escaping, riding down the highway with slug guns over our shoulders.

Well, next thing you know, there's the police, the owner of the shop, Mum, Lefty's adopted dad, and a few other people looking on. We both knew we were gunna cop it.

We never get charged; get told off though, and I reckon Lefty'll cop a hell of a flogging from his adopted dad. My beautiful mum held herself with that quiet dignity again.

WHERE YA GOING?

RICHARD 1: I'm fourteen now. It's the second time I try and leave Portland. It's later. Me and Mum had a blue. It was a big blue.

RICHARD 5: Yeah. There comes a day when most boys leave home. Find a job and find my feet.

RICHARD 4: And I think the blue was—I think I, ah—truth be known, Dad had died years before and no-one talked about it.

RICHARD 1: I'm leaving. 'Mum,' I said, 'I'm leaving'.

MUM: Okay.

RICHARD 4: Well, that shocked me.

RICHARD 1: I pack a bag and walk out the front door. It's raining. That slow, lazy, cold rain. Steady and cold. I walk down the driveway. I hear the front door open and I'm thinking she's gunna ask me to come back.

MUM: Don't forget your bloody culture.

RICHARD 1: 'Oh.' I keep walking, my back as straight as I can make it. The next thing I hear that front door—my hopes light up again.

MUM: And don't you cross no union picket line neither.

RICHARD 3: I'm hitchhiking out of town, it's cold and wet and dark. I walk out of Portland and a bloke picks me up and drops me just east of Narrawong. I walk again and walk past a big house—its lights are on and I can smell tucker. I didn't realise it then, but thirty years later I came back and bought that house. Home. Me and the bank own it now; we sort of went halvsies in it—

A truck's coming up, lights flashing through the rain, and it pulls up with a gunning of the engine, air brakes and splashing water.

I am runnin' up to the cab and opening the door and looking in, a wild-eyed bloke's lit up by a passing car.

TRUCK DRIVER: Get in, mate. You want a bloody lift or not?

RICHARD 1: I climb in and put my bag at my feet and hug my guitar for comfort; and then I look around the cab. The truck's already moving.

In between changing gears, the truckie skulls a stubbie, throws it on the floor and grabs another one, opening it and then grabbing a bottle and throwing two tablets down his throat. The truck charges through the night, rain pouring.

TRUCK DRIVER: [*looking hard at* YOUNG RICHARD] You an Abo, are ya?

[*Driving on*] I was in Vietnam with an Abo; knew a couple more in the army.

RICHARD 1: I nod—Abo—army—the truck slews through a bend and the rain hits the window hard. He takes another drink.

TRUCK DRIVER: Where ya going?

YOUNG RICHARD: Melbourne. Find a job. Help me mum.

TRUCK DRIVER: I know where the Abos drink. I'm going past. I'll drop ya there.

RICHARD 1: We drive through the night, and he talks a bit, tells me about the war, I ask him if he was scared—

TRUCK DRIVER: Yeah.

RICHARD 1: He keeps drinking, keeps taking his tablets, and I eventually stop cuddling my guitar. I must've dozed off cos I am dreaming of war, trucks and old Kooris. I wake up as the truck stops. The truck driver's shaking me and he points down a sparsely lit city street. We are in Melbourne.

TRUCK DRIVER: [*pointing*] The Abos are down there.

RICHARD 1: I look down the street but can't see nothing.

TRUCK DRIVER: [*a bit gentler*] Head straight down the street and you'll come to a park. They'll be there.

RICHARD 1: I head down the street and eventually I can see the park. The rain eases off a bit and I can see forty-four-gallon drums full of fire and people standing around them, high-rise flats like ugly cliff faces behind them.

I walk in and a couple look at me.

UNCLE: What's your name, boy?

YOUNG RICHARD: Richard Frankland, I'm a Saunders.

UNCLE: You Chrissie Saunders' boy, are ya?

YOUNG RICHARD: Yeah.

UNCLE: Well, come over here and get warm. I know your mum. What you doing down here?

YOUNG RICHARD: Come to find out about me dad.

UNCLE: Dicky Frankland? That your dad? Well, he was a good bloke, your dad. You know, tomorrow you can go and see Aunty Eleanor, she was good mates with your dad. You play much guitar?

RICHARD 1: The night goes on. I am safe. I sing the one song I wrote, and learn a few others. We all sing and giggle, someone yells some / stuff.

RICHARD 4: Shut your black hole.

RICHARD 1: Then I sleep.

The next day, all the white city people avoid the park. I'm not sure what those whitefellas are seeing, but all I can see are old uncles, aunties, cousins, stockmen, cook hands, labourers, storytellers and sometimes, if you look real hard, an old magic man.

RUNNING INTO THE WILLY-WILLY

RICHARD 5: Later. We're about three thousand k's in. Me and Mum. Yeah, I'd gone back home. Now I'm outside of a town on the Nullarbor somewhere, hungry, walking—been up to Broome for my sister's wedding, hitchhiked to Perth, slept under a tree at the Kalgoorlie turn-off. We'd lost our house in Portland, but most of the family's in Canberra so we're heading there. Things hadn't turned out so we'd left Broome with no money. Not a zac, not a brass razoo. I am the man. I am fifteen. It's 1979. We walk and walk and walk.

Here the land seems to go on forever. And I, I've lost everything. Got nothing. Can't even get a feed. No money. No blankets. And I am not sure why, but—I have this canvas bag full of my songs, poems, stories. And so I, I just walk into the bigness—Mum's watching—and I pull it all out and throw it as hard as I can.

From nowhere a willy-willy comes and picks it up mid-flight and grabs it all and whizzes it around. Mum yells, 'No!' and runs into the willy-willy.

Her hair's flinging about, whipped up, down, to the side. She's yelling and snatching it all back from the wind. It was like she was challenging nature itself. And she snatches the stuff, the songs, the poems, and the rest.

I am breathless, watching. The willy-willy passes, off into the distance, a whirl of dust, fearless in its journey. Mum stands there, tears falling, hair everywhere, handfuls of my writings. Without a word I take them from her and stuff them back in my bag. Dunno what else to do with 'em. Decide that I gotta keep writing though. Gotta get out of here first and find myself another job.

END OF ACT ONE

ACT TWO

HARD MEN

RICHARD 3: I do two stints at the army. Army Reserve, then regular army. Still two stints. Don't forget that the last bloke awarded a VC was a reservist. Anyway, meet a bloke called Danny. Don't even know where I met him.

DANNY: If you come up to Orange I'll get you some work. Good job. No problem.

RICHARD 3: So off I go. I am sixteen. 1980. I go up there. It's pretty hard up there, places like Condobolin and stuff. For tough, hard men. I fight a redneck in a carpark—park beside a pub in Orange. I flogged him.

RICHARD 4: Hah. Orange. I am the chairperson of the Orange Aboriginal Corporation.

RICHARD 3: One of the first. Fighting resettlement, networking locals, act as a voice—

But we had to change the name; there's no such thing as Orange Aboriginals.

Orange is racist, but I'm an apprentice, a glazier. You cut glass and you go and fix broken windows. Or you make shower screens or aluminium windows and—

RICHARD 5: I am in the Army Reserve—17 RNSWR—and I am living in Orange, and like any seventeen-year-old, I thought I was flash.

ANNA: You're a deadly lookin' fella.

RICHARD 5: She's from out west. Her name is Anna. She's got long black hair, a full body, really dark skin and eyes that touch my soul. She's the type of woman that could dress in a hessian bag and look good.

ANNA: You better believe it.

RICHARD 5: We never even kissed or held hands, but my heart was gone. She was unattainable. Complete. Even in this world of danger for blackfellas, she was assured. Strong. Complete.

So one weekend she goes away with her mates and I go bush with the Army Reserve, and on Monday morning, sunlight's golden through the window, and over gentle cups of tea, they tell me that she's died. Accidental overdose. I ran all day, and somewhere, I find the night, or the night finds me, and I'm looking for her, in the clouds and in the stars, looking for all the things that she said I could be.

RICHARD 3: I wake up and I am a regular full-time soldier—ECN 343—an infantry soldier with the First Platoon of A Company of the First Battalion of the Royal Australian Regiment.

SOLDIERS: [*all other* RICHARDS] Sir.

RICHARD 5: Go to Wagga. Train for three months. Up to Townsville. For the operational deployment force—ODF.

I was hoping there would be a war. I'd be safer. You at least knew who hated you.

ECN 343

ALL *get changed into army gear.*

RICHARD 5: So we're out bush and I'm with a mate, a man who I thought was a close mate—we'd shared 'hoochies' [*tents*], ration packs, beer, and our last quid together—his girlfriend had gone out with my cousin. But he says:

ARMY MATE: Nah, she'd never fuck a coon.

RICHARD 5: I am marching. We are all marching. We march up and we march down and we get yelled at. Then we run. Then we march. Then we pull rifles apart. Then we march. They even regulate when we have to do a cooney.

RICHARD 2: True!

> Black cat piddled in the white cat's eye
> Black cat piddled in the white cat's eye
> Black cat piddled in the white cat's eye
> And the white cat didn't give a fuck.

RICHARD 5: I think—I, I have no life skills, except survival.

RICHARD 3: There's no off button.

RICHARD 5: I don't drink and don't smoke.

RICHARD 4: I give up everything.

RICHARD 3: I just train.

RICHARD 5: I get up in the middle of the night and run fifteen k's. So I am fit like, um, I, I just train.

Rarriwuy Hick and Tiriki Onus in Malthouse Theatre's 2014 production.
(Photo: Pia Johnson)

RICHARD 2: All I did was train.

> Black cat piddled in the white cat's eye
> Black cat piddled in the white cat's eye
> Black cat piddled in the white cat's eye
> And the white cat didn't give a fuck.

RICHARD 5: It's um—it's um—it's waiting, it's hot and it's waiting. It's waiting for choppers. It's wanting a red alert. It's wanting to be ODF. It's wanting to smell gunpowder. It's wanting the chaos of war because the chaos of civilian life is too much. And it's alcohol and it's partying hard and then it's no drinking and training and then it's being recommended for specialist courses and laughing at them and rebelling and not rebelling. It's standing on the roof of a car with the choke on full, going around a main road. It's doing a hundred and twenty kilometres an hour on the back wheel of a motorbike through town. It's pushing a bikie in the back while he's having a / piss—

BIKIE: Piss / off …

RICHARD 5: It's the top Brigade martial arts expert challenging you off-base in front of everyone, going all Bruce Lee, wanting to teach the coon a lesson and me just laughing. I drop him.

RICHARD 3: *Bang!*

RICHARD 5: Then stand over him saying, 'You seen him kick me!'

RICHARD 3: *Bang!*

RICHARD 5: You know? It's insanity.

RICHARD 3: It's everything that every man wants to be and everything every man wants to hate.

RICHARD 2: The uniform is a like a superhero suit. It allows you to be more than normal.

RICHARD 4: I want to be in a war.

RICHARD 2: The enemy doesn't matter.

> Black cat piddled in the white cat's eye
> Black cat piddled in the white cat's eye
> Black cat piddled in the white cat's eye
> And the white cat didn't give a fuck.

RICHARD 5: We're all out on the piss, we aren't meant to be getting too pissed, we're on ODF—that's Operational Deployment for you civvies—we are on call, in case there's a war somewhere that we have to go to, we have to be ready to go, sober, ready, professional soldiers. But hey, a soldier's gotta do what a soldier's gotta do, and sometimes a beer is what we gotta do.

　　We're all at a table; someone's birthday; we're all aggressive.

ALL: Grrrrr.

RICHARD 5: Like mad pirates full of piss and vinegar.

ALL: Grrrrr.

SOLDIER 1: What are we doing tonight?

YOUNG RICHARD: Drinking!

SOLDIER 1: Where?

SOLDIER 2: Scums! [*A nightclub*]

SOLDIER 3: Later / that's later—

SOLDIER 1: The / Seaview!

SOLDIER 2: Nah, there's no band on.

SOLDIER 3: So what are we doing tonight?

SOLDIER 4: I've got it! Let's go boong bashing!

RICHARD 5: Everything is quiet, another world quiet, everyone wants to go boong bashing, except me, cos I *am* a boong! Everything is in slow motion for an eon of a split second.

RICHARD 3: They're all talking, but I can't hear them, all I hear is a roaring in my ears.

RICHARD 4: And then everything is loud, hard and fast.

RICHARD 5: Think about family. Think about Anna. What if she'd lived? Would I be here?

RICHARD 3: *Bang!*

RICHARD 5: I hit him so fucking hard and fast that his boots become level with my eyes. Out of the corner of my eye I see a bloke standing and I drop him hard.

RICHARD 3: *Bang!*

RICHARD 2: I turn quick and I hear myself saying:

RICHARD 5: Well, *I'm* a fucking boong, ya arseholes, come on, come on!

RICHARD 3: And I drop another one.

RICHARD 5: *Bang!*

RICHARD 2: Blood is dripping from my knuckles

RICHARD 4: Wasn't I meant to be in some foreign country fighting and dying with these blokes at my side?

RICHARD 1: ANZAC spirit.

YOUNG RICHARD: Come and die, you fuckers, come on! Did you hear what I said, mother fuckers, come on!
Black cat piddled in the white cat's eye
Black cat piddled in the white cat's eye
Black cat piddled in the white cat's eye
And the white cat didn't give a fuck.

FIFTY-FOUR DOLLARS IN MY POCKET

RICHARD 5: So, um, I, it's 1986, Bob Hawke, that banana republic fella Paul Keating, the Accord, *Crocodile Dundee*—hah! Leave the army—medical. All fucked up. Honourable discharge. Go to Geelong, partner has a baby, gets pregnant again, and I have fifty-four dollars in my pocket, an old shirt in my rucksack and a third of a tank of petrol and, um, we got nothin'.

RICHARD 2: So we book into a caravan park; and to save money on petrol I walk around lookin' for work.

RICHARD 4: And I am probably walking fifteen to twenty k's a day, um, just going to the factories and asking for work.

RICHARD 5: I end up on the boats with a bloke called Tubby who was from Portland—Paul Jobe.

RICHARD 1: They work us bloody hard.

RICHARD 5: My muscles are screaming after five days at sea, I am staggering with tiredness, but they give me five hundred dollars

RICHARD 1: and I take it in to the real estate agents and I am swaying—sea legs—and I say:

RICHARD 5: Look, I'm not drunk—we want a flat.

RICHARD 4: So we get into the flat, no furniture, except a mattress, six hours I gotta get back out to sea, week at a time. Need the money.

RICHARD 2: Came back—twelve-four hours unloading and then going again—and working and working and she's pregnant and, um, she's gettin' crook and, ah, get a job cuttin' steel close to home.

RICHARD 3: Out at sea we're lifting fifty- to a hundred-kilo bins of fish, but in this place, you aren't allowed to lift anything above fifteen kilos, and so I don't … and I am late to work one day, but I ring / up:

YOUNG RICHARD: Look, my partner is haemorrhaging; I really need to go to hospital—

STEEL BOSS: Oh, today she's haemorrhaging.

RICHARD 2: And, ah, so take her up to hospital and, um, then go to work, but they call me in, then they / sit me down—

STEEL BOSS: Oh look, we think it's just that thing your people do: Not turn up.

YOUNG RICHARD: But I rang you.

You got kids? How far would you go for your kids?

STEEL BOSS: Don't make it worse for yourself—

YOUNG RICHARD: This is a dog act.

If your missus was bleeding, what would you do? Would you be here? Or at the hospital?

STEEL BOSS *mutters about this being the best thing for him, etc.*

YOUNG RICHARD: No. I'm just asking you, mate.

RICHARD 2: My partner came good, but I got fired.

RICHARD 1: The unions then weren't much chop for blackfellas.

RICHARD 5: Later. Tramway Hotel, North Fitzroy.

PUB DRUNK: I know your breed better than you do, boy.

RICHARD 5: And, um—and I slam him,

RICHARD 3: *Bang!*

RICHARD 5: I hurt him … you know, I literally punch him the length of the bar, keep him in the air with my fists—and he's lying on the ground and I backhand him till he wakes up. And it's like—I look at him and he's pissed himself. Blood pissing out of him. Keening. And I think, 'Fuck, Jesus, is this what a warrior is? This is what I am. Big-time fuckin' warrior.' I walk outside and look up at the stars—

RICHARD 4: I guess I reckon every man has it. I reckon there's something that sits right down here. I feel the anger come from there, just above your pubic bone almost. It comes up and it just consumes you. It's like going into battle. The old Scots and the Vikings used to have the berserkers.

RICHARD 2: It's an almost abject lack of fear, but it's not scary. Chaos is normal—juggling hunger, family, work. It's all about survival—

RICHARD 4: You look at someone and you've got nothing to lose.

A FUCKING MAELSTROM

RICHARD 5: I do a couple of stints on the *Margaret Philippa*. Tough gig, but she's a beauty—eighty-six foot, steel, federation green and white, the bridge up forward, big back deck, massive net drum, two winches the size of small cars, steel cables that could take a hundred tonne plus of pressure.

RICHARD 4: We fish the Bass Strait, around King Island. Gemfish, blue grenadier—

RICHARD 2: Orange roughy. Fishing at night—

RICHARD 4: Sea's as black as Satan's ring.

RICHARD 2: Twelve other vessels, or more, shooting their nets away, everyone wary of the other.

RICHARD 1: No rules, no safety gear and you go in that water and you're dead in minutes—

RICHARD 3: Hell yeah!

RICHARD 5: Then, pinned up! Net's stuck on the bottom and a storm's brewing. Every other boat runs for cover.

TUBBY: Get the deck cleared. Get those fucking fish below. How is it?

YOUNG RICHARD: We're stuck hard, boss.

RICHARD 5: Tubby's bouncing the boat back and forth, Bob's working the winches trying to get the net loose from the bottom—it's probably two miles down—all before the storm hits.

TUBBY: Two hands, two fish!

RICHARDS 1 & 4: [*together*] We are!

RICHARD 2: The engine's screaming, the cables're pulling so tight if they snap they'll cut you in half; and the storm's shifting, swinging round behind us.

TUBBY: Two hands, two fucking fish!

RICHARD 4: A hundred miles out to sea and the storm hits. Huge troughs. Little willy-willies across the top of the waves. [*Angling his hand steeply*] We're like that. Waves coming straight over the stern. It's a fucking maelstrom—

If I was in a perfect storm out in Bass Strait there was no better skipper, no better man than Tubby, Paul Jobe. He'd been in the South Americas, maybe worked for an international intelligence organisation, maybe he hadn't—think he was gammonin' about that—he'd owned a pub, started a garbage company, successful, left his family comfortable. Good bloke, hard head, soft heart.

And for me he was always there. Gave me a job three times—each time when I was dead broke. White guy. We got on cos we were hard men.

Net's free of the bottom. Storm hits hard but, all the other boats had run for cover, but, as Tubby says:

TUBBY: Been in worse.

FIFTY STITCHES IN HER THROAT

RICHARDS 3 & 5: [*together*] Still, me and the missus're broke.

RICHARD 3: Fuck it. It's the mid-80s. *Crocodile Dundee 2*—the one with Ernie Dingo as the blackfella. And I won't take the dole. No way. Chaos juggling work, feeding the family, people coming and going—

Get a job interview. So I go down to the dole office and say:

Can I borrow some money? I don't want a dole cheque, I just want some money for petrol. I'll pay it back.

Get the money and, ah, get the job.

Aboriginal Legal Service. You have to pay a third of your own petrol and a third of your own phone bill. And you are on call twenty-four-seven for the whole state, but they pay you two hundred and something dollars a week.

Then investigator/field officer, get appointed to Royal Commission into Black Deaths in Custody, 1988. Ha! Tall ships. Bicentenary. Fireworks. And it's probably the worst job I ever done in my life. For a long time I was the only indigenous employee for some two and a half states. The first wage they offer me was eighteen thousand dollars per annum. The second was twenty-eight thousand. I receive no training. My role is to locate witnesses, take statements from both black and white people, and to talk to other interested parties of the Commission's proceedings.

RICHARD 5: And sometimes you wear a suit, because it's a voice game now, and who's got the most power. And they're all scared—cops and screws—of a Royal Commission. So you walk down a hallway [*clicking his fingers*] and there's three or four governors, there's all these guards, all around you, and you stop. [*He stops clicking.*]

And you adjust your suit. And you start walking again. [*Clicking his fingers*] You show them you've got the power.

And you get into that room with that woman, and you throw them all out, and you are holding her in your arms, she's crying, there's fifty stitches in her throat and another fifty or so in each arm, and all the time you've got no power to get her out; and a clear fluid from her body leaks down into your suit, and you drive home and you have to have a shower with your suit on because the fluid has stuck the suit to your body.

Ninety-nine deaths investigated, sixty in police custody. I work on a huge mob of them. Seven in detail: three were elders, one had a young family, three were stolen generation, one was an adolescent, one they beat so hard his heart was lying on his spine.

And as you're driving you look around at all the white faces around you and you're thinking, how can I grab them by the back of the head and run them through my life. And they don't know that I'm going to a funeral every second week.

RICHARD 3: Wish I was back on the boats.

RICHARD 5: When you investigate a death in custody for a Royal Commission you know how much a person weighed when they were born. You know their traditional lands, and language.

RICHARD 1: You know their family members.

RICHARD 2: You read every report available.

RICHARD 4: You read a diary, if they had one.

RICHARD 2: You see their paintings.

RICHARD 1: You hold their family members while they cry and they hold you while you cry.

RICHARD 2: You learn the rhythm of their life.

RICHARD 4: You see the scars on their soul and being.

RICHARD 5: If I investigate a death I know secrets,

RICHARD 3: I know secrets that I will never, never ever tell anybody.

RICHARD 5: As a man, I got to see the world through a mother's tears, which is a horrific sight for a male.

RICHARD 3: It's strangely beautiful, but it is absolutely wonderfully sad.

RICHARD 5: I discover that grief is fundamentally love.

RICHARD 3: I meet mothers who call me their son's names, and I let them. I'd pretend I was their son while we had a cup of tea.

RICHARD 5: I read Watchhouse Book reports which said, about a man who died in custody—

RICHARD 2: 'A good bloke for an Abo'.

RICHARD 5: Good bloke for an Abo.

RICHARD 3: Wish I was back on the boats.

RICHARD 5: There was one Koori guy. He was eleven years old when he was taken. They took him and all his brothers. Ten years later they came back and they took, not the sisters, but the sons of the sisters.

So two generations of men in the one family are gone, by the one welfare body.

Malcolm was locked up at eleven—boys home, then various prisons—for seventeen of his twenty-nine years, initially for 'stealing' a pushbike and for 'improper and incompetent guardianship'—his mum had just died—and he was free a total of just seventeen months over those seventeen years in prison.

At Malabar Assessment Unit he's put into a cell, a very small cell. Malcolm draws a picture of a hill with a pathway leading up it and a cross at the top and two large gates. And then he puts a paintbrush into his sleeve, walks past the guard to the toilet, and slams the paintbrush into his left eye. Bang! And he was dead.

SONG: 'Malcolm Smith'

RICHARD 5: *Was a Koori was Malcolm Smith*
Was a reason did what he did
Was a boy who took a bike
Was a system that took his life

How did he die?
Did he hear the mopoke cry?
No guilt, no shame
Just got locked up again

Black boy pedals a bike
Laughs cos he loves his life
Policeman come and say he bad
Lock him up and now he's dead

How did he die?
Did he hear the mopoke cry?
No guilt, no shame
Just got locked up again

Tears fallin' years gone by
Don't want to hear you cry
It's hurtin' me so bad
I knew Malcolm, Malcolm's dead

How did he die?
Did he hear the mopoke cry?
No guilt, no shame
Just got locked up again
Locked up again
Locked up again.

ONTO THE FLOOR

RICHARD 5: The cops had been watching me—a trained soldier—come back.

RICHARD 1: Back, just after I'd got out of the army, fifteen coppers stumble through my door.

RICHARD 5: I had called them the night before.

RICHARD 1: Partner'd seen a prowler hanging around. I told them I'd got me rifle out.

RICHARD 5: I could smell them coming. I had the partner hide the kids. And I unlatched the front door. I peeled off. Naked. Throw the coppers off.

RICHARD 4: And fifteen coppers hit the door hard.

RICHARD 2: But I'd already unlatched it.

RICHARD 5: They fell down flat.

RICHARD 3: Got up, embarrassed.

RICHARD 4: I just look at 'em and say:

YOUNG RICHARD: Who's first? I love fucking white boys.

COP 1: Get on the floor, you black prick.

COP 2: Get down. Smart-arse.

COP 3: You. Stand there like this [*Puts hands behind their head*].

COP 4: Get on the floor.

COP 2: Fucking get on the floor.
COP 3: You deaf or something?
COP 1: Get on the floor, you black cunt.

WAS I RESISTING?

RICHARD 3: I've cleaned out a few pubs by myself. Like flogged a heap of blokes.

I just remember hating myself after smashing people. It wasn't even a sense of victory, it was like—Fuck, you know, what am I? Some type of animal? And it was—was I the problem? Or was I, you know, resisting? Or was I just an arsehole? Like it was—that you know, it was—you're gonna die, like—I'd just seen hell ten times over and … you don't know whether you're insane; you don't know what's real about the world anymore.

AGITATORS

RICHARD 5: And I remember, back, this old blackfella who was gonna be locked up for two months for spitting at his boss.
RICHARD 4: Well, this blackfella, Percy Neal, the Chair of Yarrabah Aboriginal Council in North Queensland, appealed but the appeal court turned a two-month sentence into six months hard labour.
RICHARD 5: As he's being sentenced the Queensland magistrate says:
MAGISTRATE 1: Violence is something which has crept into Aboriginal communities. I blame your type for this growing hatred of black against white …
MAGISTRATE 2: The majority of genuine Aboriginals do not condone this behaviour.
MAGISTRATE 3: They live a happy life, and it is only the likes of yourself that upset the harmonious running of these communities. You are an agitator and a stirrer.
RICHARD 4: Neal took it to the High Court and, well, Justice Lionel Murphy said:
JUSTICE MURPHY: If he is an agitator, he is in good company.
RICHARD 4: Many of the great religious and political figures of history have been agitators, and human progress owes much to the their efforts, and the many who are unknown.

RICHARD 3: As Oscar Wilde aptly pointed out, 'Agitators are a set of interfering, meddling people, who come down to some perfectly contented class of the community and sow the seeds of discontent amongst them.

RICHARD 1: 'That is the reason why agitators are so absolutely necessary.

RICHARD 5: 'Without them, in our incomplete state, there would be no advance towards civilisation.'

RICHARDS 2, 3, 4 & 5: [*together*] Mr Neal is entitled to be an agitator.

RICHARD 1: Agitators are a set of interfering, meddling people, who come down to some perfectly contented class of the community and sow the seeds of discontent amongst them. That is the reason why agitators are so absolutely necessary.

SONG: 'Lawbreaker'

RICHARD 3: *Lawbreaker*
What laws have you broken?

Lawbreaker, oh yeah
What laws have they made?

Do they call you
Those people of dispossession?

Were you a healer born
A soldier soldier-made?

Do they call you people of dispossession
With these laws they made?

Are you a healer born
A soldier soldier-made?

Two hundred years
Is a long long time
Two hundred years
I've been crying all the time

Two hundred years
What is yours, what is mine
Two hundred years
Ain't no more cryin' this time.

HANGING POINTS

RICHARD 4: Eighteen months after the Commission. I'm twenty-seven. I'm lying on the lounge room floor of my house—

RICHARD 2: And it's like a wall breaks inside me, and I am writing all these poems—

RICHARD 4: And I write them in big letters, keep writing them on beer coasters, pizza boxes, old notepads and diaries, napkins.

RICHARD 3: And I write and I write, and in twenty minutes I must have written twenty poems, like they'd been sitting there waiting. Sometimes you hit a wall in your life—life slaps you down, you've got to get up and slap it back.

During the following lines, the rest of the RICHARDS *whisper— each reciting a distinct stanza of Richard Frankland's poetry.*

RICHARD 5: I end up having a lot of nightmares for a while. I close my eyes and I see the faces of the dead, the bodies in the morgue, the tears of the families …

I remember heat stroke—just before I left the army—training up in the high ranges in Queensland, and a black medic, Danny Williams, is sitting on my chest punching me. 'Don't you die, Franko.' And I was slipping off to the left into a world that was all quiet and warm and there was a pinprick of light way off in the distance. No pain, no chaos.

RICHARD 1: I see the mothers' tears, the grief, the sadness—

RICHARD 5: I wake up and see hanging points in my house. I wake up and I see these hanging points in my bedroom, and I see them in my lounge room, kitchen, backyard; and they call out to you. Not that you ever do anything, but they call out to you.

I wake up and I identify the hanging points: bedroom, lounge room, kitchen.

RICHARDS 5 & 3: When I wake up in the morning
I say to myself
Don't put your hand on the gun
When I wake up
Don't touch the rope
In the morning

When the sunlight's golden
Don't
The sun is coming in through the window.

THE DIRT AND THE SHOVEL

RICHARD 5: A little later, I can't see anything but sky, dirt and a shovel. I am digging my oldest sister's grave. My mate George is here. He was her mate too; there are some cousins, an uncle, others. Sometimes I think I can hear her.

RICHARD 3: We bury her out at Condah Mission. She is there with our people. At the end of the service I am holding a shovel up by her grave and offer it to family, mates:

RICHARD 4: the first bloke to take the shovel is a bloke called Barney. He is a close friend, a brother;

RICHARD 2: men and women line up to bury her, to pay final respects. I go home to Mum's place and this song falls out of me.

SONG: 'Soft Memories' (A)

RICHARD 4: *Soft memories calling*
The winds of time
Blow through the air

RICHARD 5: *I heard you calling*
I looked around
But you weren't there

ALL: *How can I change*
The way I feel?
Losing you
Just wasn't real
To me
Wasn't real
To me.

RICHARD 1: My big sister had been hit by a drunk kid. He was riding an unregistered and unroadworthy motorbike. She was just walking across the road.

RICHARD 2: My mate Coops gives me his car and we drive home—four hours, night, I think it's raining. Big storm. She was brain dead. My heart was so alive with pain I could hardly stand it. My big sis that sung 'Night Moves'. The faceless one.

SONG: 'Soft Memories' (B)

RICHARD 4: *Time's pased me by*
　　　　I think of the special things you told me
RICHARD 5: *Try not to cry*
　　　　I wonder at the way you used to hold me
ALL: 　　*How can I change*
　　　　The way I feel?
　　　　Losing you
　　　　Just wasn't real
　　　　To me
　　　　Wasn't real
　　　　To me.

RICHARD 1: Doctors said there was no hope for her. We decide to turn off her life support system. She takes her last breath. And I can't breathe. Is that it?

　　Funny thing about death: it's all the same colour.

END OF ACT TWO

ACT THREE

THROWING A ROCK

RICHARD 5: Later, years later, I'm watching TV and I see this kid throwing a rock at a tank and I see another kid get shot. A kid.

RICHARD 4: I scab up some money, grab my mate Ralph who grabs a camera, and we jump on a plane.

RICHARD 2: Whole new vocation. And I am in the Middle East just outside of Ramallah. In the thick of it.

RICHARD 1: My pop—Old Chris Saunders—was here. Had served here.

RICHARD 5: Down the road. Gates of Jerusalem. First World War. And then, two uncles in the second. Now me, Second Intifada, 2001.

RICHARD 2: It's early morning, a piccaninny dawn, that time of morning when the light is there but the sun has not visited yet—false dawn. A man is singing. I don't know the words but his voice is beautiful and somehow peaceful, soothing. We are two storeys up. It's raining. Water is running down the street and I can't help but think how strange this looks. The land is dry, like some places back home, reminding me of another war—my war. An armoured vehicle drives up the hill and our eyes follow it. We see a woman walking in the rain and I reckon that the man singing is asking people to get up and pray.

I pray, silently, in my own way—and we are with a young boy. He has beautiful eyes; he is twelve; he's in a wheelchair and has not seen his family for weeks.

He says he misses them. Ralph puts his camera in the boy's arms and, laughing, pushes him around in his wheelchair. The boy is laughing too, especially when he comes to a mirror and sees himself in the camera in the mirror. We hear what we think are shots in the distance. There are people watching us: our interpreter, an elder and the occasional nursing staff walking through. Ralph takes the camera back, sets up for the interview.

We start. He'd been shot. How? How many times?

BOY: Five.

RICHARD 2: He shows me his scars, and although his eyes are in the body of a twelve-year-old, he is an old man.

YOUNG RICHARD: What happened?

BOY: I heard the soldiers coming and we all ran to see them.

YOUNG RICHARD: Who ran?

BOY: Me and my friends. And then I was shot. Then the soldiers came and got me and took me to the hospital. They say I won't be able to run again, or walk.

YOUNG RICHARD: Jesus.

BOY: I have not seen my mother for forty-three days. Checkpoints.

YOUNG RICHARD: Checkpoints?

BOY: She doesn't have the right passes. I miss my family.

I want to be a surgeon when I grow up.

YOUNG RICHARD: Yes.

BOY: I want to heal people, children.

YOUNG RICHARD: What's your message for the world, mate?

BOY: [*in language*] For every mother's tear and every drop of blood, let there be peace. [*Back to English*] Tell the other children, tell your children, they are killing us children here.

YOUNG RICHARD: Our eyes lock and there is silent agreement. His eyes carve themselves onto my soul. And his eyes have the same scars on them that I see in the eyes of children back home. They are the type of eyes that say, 'I've got no hope, but I'm going to keep fighting'; 'I'm really sad, but I'm going to be happy' type eyes; real 'Can I trust you?' type of eyes.

And as he spoke, I look at the monitor and, looking at this boy in the monitor, I think, I'm talking to a giant. He'd only come up to my chest, but I swear to God, I'm talking to a giant.

Later—with thirty-something tapes in my backpack, thirty-something names, should do more—I'm walking through this checkpoint, first one outside of Ramallah, Palestine, others looming, and there's a fucking modern machine-gun over there, plus this kid with a Tar 21 'Tavor', and this young soldier's looking fucking scared, panicking—me bulging backpack! The thirty-something tapes. He's thinking it could be a bomb.

And the young soldier starts hollering at me in Arabic; in Hebrew; in Russian—

My hands are up. He's pointing his gun at me.

Spot grey hair under a helmet. If I can get this other, older soldier's attention I'll be right. He'll take control. And so I don't pay the young one any attention. Though he does cock his weapon. At least three times.

Thinking fast—what don't they hear at checkpoints? ... So I start laughing. I'm just a guy with a shitty little camera and no money, standing at a checkpoint with some young soldier who might be about to shoot me. I pat my belly. Laughing. 'Bloody hill. Too steep for my big belly.'

Earlier, back earlier, the guy who owned my hotel had said don't let them get the tapes—better to die than live with the death of others. Thirty-three interviews. Thirty-three names. They'd trusted me.

Slowly I pull my passport out. The older soldier looks at it. He's laughing now too:

'Your lucky day, Australia?'

And my job is to get through this, to get more stories, voices, to have lots of voices, not just one or two, but fifty voices, a hundred voices.

There are kids dying and kids killing kids. And I think, what the friggin' hell is going on here? Like how do we, how can we, stop a war? Mothers are losing their children. We're all bleeding. Can't you see what I see? And it's Christmas.

YOU'RE SICK

RICHARD 4: And it's Christmas. I am near the southern Mexican border. It's 2002. I'm almost forty. Am too old for this shit. Getting more voices for my backpack. Stories of survivors.

The war here is silent and deadly. Forty-seven people, praying, had been murdered by paramilitaries a couple of years before. Tiny place called Acteal in the Mexican state of Chiapas.

Every year the locals re-enact the massacre. Thousands go. Survivors, perpetrators, families of victims. These victims are known as martyrs. One survivor says:

SURVIVOR: 'We need to pass through the suffering again and again. We offer our lives and blood for peace. We continue to resist, that is why we stay, even if the shots keep coming.'

RICHARD 4: Their capacity for forgiveness is extraordinary. And still they pray:

SURVIVOR & RICHARD 4: [*together*] 'I will comfort those who mourn, bestow beauty instead of ashes, bind the broken-hearted, release prisoners from the darkness, repair the desolation of generations ...'

RICHARD 4: It's Isaiah 61 ... the exaltation of the afflicted ... And I want them to come home and film our children, who are killing themselves, who are the walking dead, who are stuck on drugs and alcohol, who believe they don't fit into society. We gotta create a big international filming-without-borders program. Now there's a job.

DOCTOR: Mr Frankland, you're sick.

RICHARD 4: And I am back, back in Australia, and I am at the doctors' clutching a copy of the *Geelong Advertiser*. I love that paper. And I nod. 'The flu?' I say.

DOCTOR: Hmmmm.

RICHARD 4: He punches something into the computer and reads for a moment. I hear this magpie warbling.

DOCTOR: Your immune system is shot—

RICHARD 4: I start sweating again, but I feel cold—bloody freezing. And I am thinking of another doctor, all the doctors back in Mexico. Back in the place that put paid to my immune system.

I am real crook—

We go to doctor after doctor. Street doctors. Then we go to the hospital and there are some earnest young doctors there, all worried, but 'Not enough medication' they say.

My mate finds me this proper doctor, fifty dollars US a visit.

MEDICO: Typhoid.

YOUNG RICHARD: Nah, I had the shots.

MEDICO: [*giving him a handful of prescriptions and a handful of tablets*] Doesn't matter. Typhoid.

Beat.

YOUNG RICHARD: Yeah, I say. I think: What fucking next?

MEDICO: Drink six litre water a day or you die.

YOUNG RICHARD: I nod. Fuck.

MEDICO: You shit blood, you die.

RICHARD 4: And I am shitting so much that I reckon I could have blocked Melbourne city sewerage twice over and still had some to spare—

MEDICO: You understand?

YOUNG RICHARD: I nod.

MEDICO: You shit blood you die. You drink water or you die.

DOCTOR: How're your sugar levels?

YOUNG RICHARD: What?

DOCTOR: Mr Frankland, how are your sugar levels?

YOUNG RICHARD: Fuck. Geelong. Huh? Not sure. Haven't checked for a bit.

DOCTOR: We need to get your management plan in place.

YOUNG RICHARD: I nod.

RICHARD 4: But back, back in my Mexican motel room, with typhoid and Doctor You-Shit-Blood-And-You-Die coming to see me every other day, I lose thirteen kilos in ten days: sweating, hallucinating, laughing at myself, and shitting, lots of shitting. Cooney everywhere.

Sleep, wake, shovel tablets down my throat, skull water, freeze, shake uncontrollably, stinkin' hot showers till I stop shaking, then back to bed, more sleep. Until I wake up and I see them.

Sitting on the walls: four, five, six, twenty, thirty, countless. They are as large as my closed fist—black, evil-looking bastards of things. Long furry legs, hard shells, and watching me. Then they all take off and fly around the room. I hold the scream back in my throat. Don't acknowledge the fucks, they don't exist. Fuck 'em.

One flies off the wall almost in slow motion and lands on the part of my throat where my neck joins my body. It lands heavy and I feel all eight or ten or however many fucking legs it has dig in. I want to grab it and throw it off my neck and smash it and all of its mates and then run screaming down the road to the nearest bar and get fucking gloriously drunk on tequila and pretend that fucking typhoid and big black flying bugs don't exist.

Fuck you and your ugly mates. But later, convinced I hear soldiers coming, I start hiding the tapes. Then I start slipping off … to the left, but I ain't gonna die; I can see my daughter's face glowing—And then, later, in Mexico City, I cover a nurse in me blood, but—

DOCTOR: Mr Frankland? Hey? Management plan?

RICHARD 4: Back home the doctor gives me Keflex, same as I had in Mexico.

DOCTOR: God forbid—

RICHARD 4: It's something he says a lot.

DOCTOR & MEDICO: [*together*] God forbid you get sick.

END OF ACT THREE

ACT FOUR

KING TIDE

SONG: 'My Roads'

RICHARD 1: *Hey yeh yeh yeh*
RICHARD 4: So I go back home.
Hey yeh yeh yeh
RICHARD 3: And I go back home.
Hey yeh yeh yeh
RICHARD 1: Home's always Portland and Heywood. The dusty smell of Heywood in summer; and Portland winters, we're always wet, always cold, always breathing in real cold air from the sea.
Hey yeh yeh yeh
RICHARD 4: Once the sea's in you, she calls out to you. A Koorreen, blowing hard, a south wind straight from the Antarctic.
Hey yeh yeh yeh
RICHARD 3: I'm walking over to the beach just east of Portland, Narrawong. See Lefty Wright and his kids collecting sharks' teeth on the beach. He's come home.
Hey yeh yeh yeh
RICHARD 1: Doctor said I'm not meant to be walking too far, or even by myself. But I can't help it.
Hey yeh yeh yeh
RICHARD 4: It's like that old ocean—Nyamat—is calling out to me.
Hey yeh yeh yeh
RICHARD 3: A king tide's coming in—I feel the Korreen on my face, gentle-like, and I think, whoa, if I had a turn here, I'd just float out to sea and no-one would know. In a strange way it would be beautiful.

I should die here. Home. I been wanting to come home. I'd nearly died in a few places, some of them far away. But I want to come home; not to die, but to live. I want to live. I want to live at home.
Hey yeh yeh yeh.

SHE WASN'T LOST

RICHARD 5: I had been looking for a while now.

RICHARD 2: For my little sister. She was taken a long time ago.

RICHARD 1: At birth. Mum might have got a hug in before they took her.

RICHARD 4: Took her from the maternity ward. I didn't even know till my older sister told me.

RICHARD 3: And my little sister—the taken one— well, she knew bugger all.

RICHARD 1: I find her.

RICHARD 3: And she wasn't lost.

RICHARD 2: I mean, I just didn't know where she was. Koori Link-Up helped.

RICHARD 5: Then a white guy in an office—he had the file.

RICHARD 3: Couldn't show me. Left it open on a desk.

RICHARD 4: Somebody had told her we were dead.

RICHARD 3: I wrote her letters. And she'd seen me on TV talking about the Commission.

RICHARD 5: She rang the office a couple of times when I was out.

RICHARD 2: Everyone was excited. I was nervous. I missed a couple of her calls, and she didn't leave a number.

RICHARD 3: I am sitting, trying to work, trying to read a file of someone who had been taken and died in jail.

RICHARD 2: Ring ring.

COLLEAGUE 1: [*into the phone*] Royal Commission …?

RICHARD 3: False alarm, just someone wanting to make an appointment to make a statement.

RICHARD 2: Silence, clock ticks, chairs creak, papers shuffle.

COLLEAGUE 2: Anyone want a cuppa?

RICHARD 3: Yes please. But I want a scotch.

    Chitchat resumes.

RICHARD 2: Ring ring.

    The phone rings. Everyone stops mid-conversation.

COLLEAGUE 1: [*into the phone*] Royal Commission …

    Silence.

Yes, yes he's here, I'll put you through.

Beat.

[*To* RICHARD 3] It's her—

RICHARD 3: I pick up the phone. I pick up the phone, I am shaking, my hands are sweating.

[*Into the phone*] G'day, Richard Frankland.

SISTER 2: Hi, it's me. Your sister. How are you?

RICHARD 3: Not bad, how are you? They wouldn't tell me about you, and I—

SISTER 2: It's okay.

RICHARD 2: We meet in a car park in Bundoora.

It's a day when it's grey, everyone around us is going on with their business—shopping, talking, stony city faces walking past— me hyper-vigilant, but seeing nothing while seeing everything.

We talk.

I marvel at how much she looks like Mum, like my other sisters. She goes back to her life, I go back to mine.

And I wait, wait for her to be ready—to come home, come home to country.

SONG: 'Mama'

RICHARD 4:   *Mama I found my sister*
　　　　　　They had taken her away
　　　　　　I found my baby sister
　　　　　　Didn't know what to say
　　　　　　It's time I took a stand
　　　　　　Fight till judgement day

　　　　　　Gonna fight
　　　　　　Gonna fight
　　　　　　Till judgement day
　　　　　　Till judgement day.

THE CROSS

RICHARD 3: This chant keeps going through my head, sorta like I'm syncing up with the tyres on the road … hah hah hah hah hah hah

… I'm humming fast along this road. Sorta dancing in the sunlight.

I keep chasing different Koori tapes in my car; they fall on the floor, in between the seats. I fight the car and the mess in the car for them … hah hah hah hah hah hah … tyres humming, chant going … sunlight … *sunlight* shining.

I am coming back from a funeral up north. Big sky country. The sun glints off the bonnet and I can see Old Brucey at the fire singing, Steven dancing, clapping those clapsticks, and I can hear that didg that Dougie's playing … hah hah hah hah hah hah … come on now, come on now … hah hah hah hah hah hah …

Tyres humming, chant going … sunlight on the bonnet … *sunlight yelling at me* … See plumes of dust in the distance. Sunlight's telling me that everything is maybe okay …

There's a church in the distance in a paddock, no trees around it, it must be Sunday, all the whitefellas are there, in their Sunday best … can't find no tape so I throw the radio on …

SONG: 'California Dreaming'

During the following, RICHARD 5 *sings lines from 'California Dreaming' between paragraphs of dialogue.*

RICHARD 5: Everything is surreal, slowed down, everything is graphic, the colours of the world have become loud, and in my spirit I am dancing across the horizon, looking down …

He sings.

I see them, the car is driving hard, tyres humming, chant going … sunlight on the bonnet … *sunlight yelling at me* … telling me that everything will be okay …

He sings.

The church is closer now.

He sings.

Pray … where do I pray? Tyres humming, didg going hard, chant going, sunlight on the bonnet … *sunlight yelling at me … Where are my sacred places to pray in?*

He sings.

I been on my spiritual knees begging, begging to end the pain of all this death, the mess, the chaos ... I've been on my spiritual knees ...

He sings.

Tyres humming, didg going hard, chant going ... sunlight on the bonnet ... *sunlight yelling at me ... Where are my sacred places?*

He sings.

During the final chorus, he stands and begins speaking in language, continuing as the song finishes, walking downstage and painting up, covering his forehead in white ochre.

IN THE OLDEST GANG IN THE WORLD

RICHARD 1: All the kids are here, all the foster kids. All gangster.

ALL: [*with crotch-grab*] Huh!

RICHARD 5: They arrive with two carers. I welcome them. My place. Portland. That place I'd gone halvsies in with the bank.

RICHARD 2: Make my own work now.

RICHARD 4: Studied. Read up. Talked with the old people. Wrote some stuff down. Cos our young people are still vulnerable. Kids are killing themselves. Kids are being removed ... Right now, it's a new stolen generation.

RICHARD 3: White man's law stops at that cattle grid. This is lore here, Aboriginal way. And this is an Aboriginal family here. We protect family. And you are *Warren Warren*—boys. I could call you *Warren Maar* if you want,—boy-men; or I can call you, and treat you, like *Maar*—men. How's it going to be?

The BOYS all nod. Their voices get deeper.

BOYS: We wanna be men.

Their eyes are guarded and downcast.

RICHARD 3: You muck up, I'll slap the black straight off you. And don't look at Mother Earth, she's not going to help you now. Gotta help yourselves.

He sees a boy throw chewing gum to the ground.

Don't throw that junk on my land. And take your hat off when you speak to me. Don't slouch, stand strong, stand proud. Got a broken leg, have ya? Don't go standing on one leg. Stand with both feet on this Gunditjmara land. Now: we're gonna work out how we relate to one another.

You are men.

Now, look at me—

They look up, their eyes are sullen, guarded. They are waiting to be hurt.

—men. *Maar.*

Take your hands out of your pockets; playing with your *boobelas*, are ya?

You are in the oldest gang in the world. You walk where fifteen hundred generations of your grandfathers and grandmothers walked. You walk in their footsteps. When you look at the stars, you see what all your grandmothers and grandfathers have seen. My children catch their first fish where fifteen hundred generations of their grandparents caught their first fish.

Now, what's fire good for?

BOY 1: Cooking.

BOY 4: Smoko—

BOY 2: Keeping warm.

BOY 3: Burning stuff.

RICHARD 3: Mmm; and for forgetting things, hiding things.

They look puzzled.

Sometimes, men get scars on their soul: from too many coffins, too many hard times. What do men do when they become too much?

BOY 3: Some drink, hey Unc?

BOY 1: Some do drugs.

BOY 2: Some—

Beat.

BOY 4: Hurt their family.

Silence. Fire crackling.

BOY 1: What do you do, Uncle?

RICHARD 3: I look at them and then back at the fire. All us men are talking business now. The fire crackles.

BOY 2: Yeah—

BOY 3: How do you get past them scars, Uncle?

Silence, waiting, fire crackling.

RICHARD 3: I whisper all them scars in my hand.

They all look. RICHARD 3 *whispers into his hand, holds it real tight, then, throws the scars in the fire.*

I let the fire hide them scars for a bit, just so I can have a little break from them. Gotta cut 'em loose for a bit. I don't want those scars to disappear forever though, I want them to come back to me, because even though they hurt, they make me who I am, who I can be.

You try. Whisper a secret in your hands. Then throw it in the fire.

At first one, then another, and then all of the boy-men whisper their scars into their hands and throw them into the fire: each one serious; each one relinquishing a burden; each one having a break from the scars from life that they carry on their souls as:

Back, back on the day my youngest was born, I almost lost her. She wasn't breathing, she's grey—midwives, doctors working furious—and when she came good I, I ... steal a moment, peel off her blankets and ... breathe my spirit into her. Whisper her, her name—means birdsong in my language, hah, in our language. Now, now she's the short but dangerous one. But that day, I, well, I think she breathed life into me; in fact all my kids breathe life into me. Father, brother, son, man. And I remember thinking I was a man at fifteen, doing the Nullarbor hungry. Me, trying to do what men do: provide, protect. Just like back on the milk crate at Bothy's.

Now come with me. Come on then.

We are going to kill some sheep.

Tim is sitting on a sheep and in his hands, a knife.

We are going to kill this sheep, then we are going to cut him up and feed some elders in town and feed ourselves.

So who wants to see this sheep die?

They all nod, mostly out of bravado.

Are you sure?

BOYS: Yeah / Awesome / Sure / 'S just chops.

They all nod confidently.

RICHARD 3: You really sure?

BOYS: Yes, Uncle.

RICHARD 3: Tim holds the knife up.

There's going to be a lot of blood.

They nod nervously.

The knife goes in. The blood flows.

BOYS: Yaaaahhhhh!

RICHARD 3: The sheep dies. The boys scatter. All of them look sickly. All look like boys again. The hard, cunning street eyes are gone. Some have been crying.

When they come back they all try to avoid looking at the dead sheep. Tim picks it up and we lift it to the hook—he starts gutting it. Nama, another feller who's here, starts gutting another. The boys gather around, interested in the gutting; the poo bag, geel bag. They can see things a little clearer.

YOU DUST YOURSELF OFF

RICHARD 1: Mum had me reading books at the age of eleven, like *Bury My Heart at Wounded Knee* and *Papillon*.

RICHARD 4: True, aye.

RICHARD 3: Banjo and Henry, Kipling and Tennyson.

RICHARD 1: And while I probably didn't understand all of those books, all of the machinations of it,

RICHARD 4: I certainly understood about the power of words, of writing it down, of keeping stories in your backpack and the quest for, um, ah, justice and equity, and that next step, if you know what I mean.

RICHARD 2: So I think Mum gave me things that she enjoyed reading. And she probably knew me better than I knew myself. She probably knew I was very much …

RICHARD 5: ah, I was very much, I was very much like my dad in a lot of ways, and I got to have that sense of social equity and justice and I wasn't always good at it because, um, I fell over a lot. But when life slaps you down, you get up and slap it back.

WE WHISTLE

RICHARD 1: My dad, he used to say, have a good sense of right and wrong. I hear him singing to me:

> DAD *sings a few lines of 'Zip-a-dee-doo-dah'.*

RICHARD 5: He died when I was six. He tried twice before he managed it. I found him once, in the sunlight, in our front door, door open. There were tablets all round him. I was so young I thought they were lollies. I went to eat them and then thought, 'Nah, they belong to him'. I picked them all up and put them in the open bottle that was beside him. I kissed him. Then, later, later there was adults everywhere.

RICHARD 1: The next time was on the Yarra Boulevard, in his car. You know death comes on a sunny day, did you know that?

RICHARD 4: I remember as everyone was crying, going into his wardrobe and finding a shirt of his that hadn't been washed. I picked it up and smelled him—he seemed to be alive still when I smelled his shirt. I drank in the smell, my tears mixing with his smell.

RICHARD 5: I'd gone looking for my dad. But I already knew. I was there.

RICHARD 2: I can still smell him today. The old people say that you can smell spirits—I can still smell my dad. If I close my eyes I can smell him; when I really need him I can smell him.

RICHARD 4: So now I am singing with my kids:

> *It's a beautiful day*
> *This day today*
> *I can hear the birds a-singing*
> *They seem to say ...*

RICHARD 2: Sometimes as I was growing up I could feel my dad there. 'Sorry,' he seems to say; 'I should have stayed,' he seems to say—but that's the way the world is sometimes.

RICHARD 1: 'Bye, Dad. One day, he moved on, I felt him move on; but he left a bit of himself for me—

DAD: Have a good sense of right and wrong, have a good sense of right and wrong:

RICHARD 1: We whistle.

END OF ACT FOUR

Tiriki Onus, Rarriwuy Hick, Paul Ashcroft, Luisa Hastings Edge and Tammy Anderson in Malthouse Theatre's 2014 production. (Photo: Pia Johnson)

EPILOGUE

MY NAME IS RICHARD

RICHARD: My name's Richard Frankland; and I'm a Greek-looking Aboriginal who's worked as a waiter in a Chinese restaurant that was owned by a white bloke who happened to be gay. Not that there's anything wrong with being white.

I also worked as a hay baler, apprentice glazier, soldier, fisherman, Royal Commission investigator and dad. It's the hardest job of all. Oh, and we've got one more thing for you …

SONG: 'Cry Freedom'

>*Yeeeeeeeaaaaaa*
>*Freedom!*

>*They don't like it*
>*When we're marching down the street*
>*Only fighting for our rights*

>*Oh, how they like to judge the things we say and do*
>*From the safety of their ivory heights*

>*You can't be wrong if you're right*
>*You can't be wrong if you're right*
>*You can't be wrong if you're right*
>*Won't you cry freedom with me?*
>*Cry freedom*

>*You can't be wrong if you're right*
>*You can't be wrong if you're right*
>*You can't be wrong if you're right*
>*Won't you cry freedom with me?*

THE END

RELATED PLAYS
FROM CURRENCY PRESS

The Drover's Wife
Leah Purcell

Winner of: Best New Australian Work, Sydney Theatre Awards (2016). Best Drama & the Victorian Prize for Literature, Victorian Premier's Literary Awards (2017)

Tarantino meets Deadwood in this full-throttle drama of our colonial past, written by the indomitable Leah Purcell. Henry Lawson's story of 'The Drover's Wife' pitted the stoic silhouette of a woman against the unforgiving Australian landscape, staring down a serpent – it's our frontier myth captured in a few pages.

In Leah's new play the old story gets a very fresh rewrite. Once again the drover's wife is confronted by a threat in her yard in Australia's high country, but now it's a man. He's bleeding, he's got secrets, and he's black. She knows there's a fugitive wanted for killing whites, and the district is thick with troopers, but something's holding her back from turning this fella in...

A taut thriller of our pioneering past, ***The Drover's Wife*** is full of fury, power and has a black sting to the tail, reaching from our nation's infancy into our complicated present.

978-1-92500-571-4, available as an ebook

Aliwa!
Dallas Winmar

This play traces the true story of three Aboriginal sisters whose mother was determined to keep her children when officials wanted to remove them following the death of their father. The story is that of the three sisters of the playwright Jack Davis.

978-0-86819-688-6

Blak Inside

This collection of six Indigenous plays from Victoria contains: ***I Don't Wanna Play House*** by Tammy Anderson, ***Conversations With the Dead*** by Richard J. Frankland, ***Enuff*** by John Harding, ***Crow Fire*** by Jadah Milroy, ***Belonging*** by Tracey Rigney and ***Casting Doubts*** by Maryanne Sam.

978-0-86819-662-6

Brothers Wreck
Jada Alberts
Winner of the Mona Brand Emerging Writer Award (2016)

On a hot Darwin morning, Ruben wakes to find his cousin Joe hanging from the house rafters. What follows is the story of a family holding itself together – as their people have done generation after generation. This play asks us: how do we deal with death? And how many other people does it take for each of us to live? Little by little, Ruben's family brings him back from the edge.

978-1-92500-513-4, also available as an ebook

Contemporary Indigenous Plays
Five plays of rich Indigenous storytelling in contemporary theatre. ***Bitin' Back*** by Vivienne Cleven, ***Black Medea*** by Wesley Enoch, ***King Hit*** by David Milroy and Geoffrey Narkle, ***Rainbow's End*** by Jane Harrison & ***Windmill Baby*** by David Milroy.

978-0-86819-795-1, also available as separate ebooks

Kill the Messenger
Nakkiah Lui

Based on a true story about a man in the author Nakkiah's suburb of Mount Druitt. One day, in unbearable pain due to undiagnosed stomach cancer, he went to the local hospital, where he was refused care. Then he went to a nearby park and hung himself. Then in Nakkiah's grandmother fell through the unmended floor of her public housing home and died. Nakkiah found herself at the centre of a story about institutional racism.

978-1-92500-537-0, also available as an ebook

Namatjira / Ngapartji Ngapartji
Scott Rankin with the Namatjira family and Trevor Jamieson (Pitjantjatjara)

Two plays. The story of Albert Namatjira (1902–1959), Australia's most famous Indigenous watercolour artist, and the story of a Pitjantjatjara family forcibly moved off their lands to make way for the testing of British atomic bombs at Maralinga.

978-0-86819-922-1, also available as separate ebooks

No Sugar
Jack Davis

The spirited story of the Millimurra family's stand against government 'protection' policies in 1930s Australia.

978-0-86819-146-1, also available as an ebook

Stolen
Jane Harrison

The story of five young Aboriginal children forcibly removed from their parents, brought up in a repressive children's home and trained for domestic service and other menial jobs. The pain, poignancy and sheer desperation of their lives is seen through the children's own eyes as they struggle to make sense of a world where they have been told to forget their families, their homes and their language. This story, awash with childlike humour, brings the history of the Stolen Generations to the stage.

978-0-86819-797-5, also available as an ebook

The Dreamers
Jack Davis

With humane irony, Jack Davis gives a painful insight into the process of colonisation and the transformation of his people. *The Dreamers* is the story of a country-town family and old Uncle Worru, who in his dying days, recedes from urban hopelessness to the life and language of the Nyoongah spirit which in him has survived 'civilisation'.

978-0-86819-454-7, also available as an ebook

The Story of the Miracles at Cookie's Table
Wesley Enoch

In the 1870's a girl is born under a tree – her birth tree. When the tree is cut down she follows it into the white man's world, working as a cook for the big house on the island. Now, generations later, a young man and his mother fight for ownership of the table. This a moving testament to culture lived, lost and found, the strength of family, adapting and gathering together.

978-0-86819-803-3, also available as an ebook

Yanagai! Yanagai!
Andrea James

Munarra is a black woman, thrown from the skies into the Dreaming so that she may heal her land, the mighty river Dhungula and her people. In the present day, the Yorta Yorta people are in court, fighting for a right to their land. Since its premiere in 2003, *Yanagai! Yanagai!* has been performed in France, the United Kingdom, the United States and the Philippines. Some of these Yorta Yorta stories are told so that they may be remembered; others are told in the hope that they never occur again.

978-1-92500-577-6, also available as an ebook

www.currency.com.au

Visit Currency Press' website now to:

- Buy your books online
- Browse through our full list of titles, from plays to screenplays, books on theatre, film and music, and more
- Choose a play for your school or amateur performance group by cast size and gender
- Obtain information about performance rights
- Find out about theatre productions and other performing arts news across Australia
- For students, read our study guides
- For teachers, access syllabus and other relevant information
- Sign up for our email newsletter

The performing arts publisher

www.ingramcontent.com/pod-product-compliance
Lightning Source LLC
Chambersburg PA
CBHW050025090426

42734CB00021B/3423